I. M. PEI
Designer of Dreams

I. M. Pei
Designer of Dreams

By Pamela Dell

CP CHILDRENS PRESS ®
CHICAGO

PHOTO CREDITS

AP/Wide World—Cover, 21, 28, 30, 32
John F. Kennedy Library—23
© Monica Liu—8, 13
Courtesy of I.M. Pei—1, 2, 3 (Evelyn Hofer), 10, 14,
    15, 16, 19, 24, 26
Root Resources—© David J. Sams, 22; © Jay Malin, 29
© Steve Rosenthal—17
SuperStock International—5, 11
UPI/Bettmann Newsphotos—7, 27, 31
Words and Pictures—© Carl Purcell, 25

DESIGN AND ELECTRONIC COMPOSITION: Biner Design

Library of Congress Cataloging-in-Publication Data

Dell, Pamela.
    I. M. Pei, designer of dreams / by Pamela Dell.
    p. cm. — (Picture story biography)
    Summary: Briefly discusses the family background,
education, and work of the Chinese-American architect
known for his creations in glass and concrete.
    ISBN 0-516-04186-X
    1. Pei, I. M., 1917–   —Juvenile literature. 2. Chinese-
American architects—Biography—Juvenile literature. [1.
Pei, I. M., 1917– . 2. Architects. 3. Chinese-Americans
—Biography.] I. Title. II. Series: Picture-story biographies.

NA737.P365D46   1993   92-36903
720'.92—dc20   CIP
[B]   AC

The Louvre, Paris

PICTURE A seventy-story skyscraper towering over downtown Hong Kong. A huge glass pyramid in front of the Louvre art museum in Paris. A glass-and-steel terminal at New York's Kennedy Airport. An elegant hotel set in a serene garden on the outskirts of Beijing, China. Can you guess what these buildings have in common?

They were all designed by the same person! All these buildings were created by I. M. Pei, one of America's greatest architects. (An architect is someone who designs buildings and supervises their construction.)

It takes a special gift to imagine and create so many different kinds of structures. You must be able to look at an empty space in a special way. You must imagine how that space would best be filled. Then you must put on paper what you see with your mind's eye. Your way of seeing the world must be unusual and imaginative.

This certainly describes I. M. Pei. For more than four decades, he has been known as a highly creative architect. His designs range from massive public buildings to intimate chapels and hotels. All his life, even as a young boy, I. M. has been interested in the architecture around him.

I. M.'s full name is Ieoh Ming, which means "to inscribe brightly" in Chinese, but he likes to be called I. M. He was born in China on April 26, 1917, in the city of Canton (now called Guangzhou). His ancestors had lived for more than six hundred years in the city of Suzhou, northwest of Shanghai.

The Pearl River, in Canton, China, around the year when I. M. Pei was born

Suzhou, China

Suzhou was an important city in the
rice and silk trades. It was also known
for its many craftsmen, scholars, and
artists. People considered the city so
wonderful that there was a saying
about it and its neighboring city: "In
heaven there is paradise; on earth,
Suzhou and Hangzhou."

I.M.'s father, Tsuyee Pei, came from a prosperous landowning family. He met his wife-to-be while he was a student at the university. Tsuyee was an ambitious young man, and he soon became a successful executive in the Bank of China. In 1914, the bank sent Tsuyee to open a new branch in Canton. There, I.M.'s mother, Lien Kwun, gave birth to a daughter, Yuen Hau. Their second child, I.M., was born in 1917.

At that time, fighting among local warlords made life dangerous in Canton. In 1918, the bank told Tsuyee to move with his family to the safety of Hong Kong, which was then governed by Great Britain. Sometimes on that long journey I.M.'s nurse, or "amah," carried him on her back.

The Pei family lived in Hong Kong for nine years. During that time, three

I. M. with his
aunt in 1920

more children were born—I.M.'s sister
Wei, and his two brothers, Kwun and
Chung. Then, in 1927, I.M.'s father
was made manager of the bank's main
office in Shanghai, and the family
returned to China.

I. M. respected his father, but he was much closer to his mother, who was more openly affectionate. Lien Kwun was a gifted flute player and a devout Buddhist. As the eldest son, I. M. had a special place in her heart. He felt free to seek her advice with his problems. On two occasions, I. M.'s mother took him on religious retreats. These

I. M. was deeply influenced by his religious retreats with his mother to Buddhist temples, such as this one in Guangzhou.

journeys were a privilege that none of I.M.'s brothers or sisters were ever asked to share.

Sadly, when I.M. was only thirteen years old, his mother died. But her love for him and their visits to the Buddhist temples left a lasting impression on I.M. The deep silence of the mountain retreat where they had stayed remained vivid in his mind.

In the summers, the Pei family journeyed to Suzhou, where many of their relatives still lived. On these trips, everyone—including I.M.—dressed traditionally, in long silk robes.

The family retreat in Suzhou was known as the Garden of the Lion Forest. The beautiful Lion Forest gardens were skillfully designed. Even as a young boy, I.M. noticed how buildings and nature were combined in the gardens. He was especially

The Garden of the Lion Forest, the Pei family retreat

impressed by the way light and
shadow played together in their
design. More than fifty years later he
would return to the Garden of the Lion
Forest. This visit would inspire his
design of the Fragrant Hill Hotel in
Beijing, China.

   Back in Shanghai, many new
buildings were under construction.
I. M. was awed by the first high-rise

building he ever saw. It was twenty-three stories high! Wherever he went, he began to be acutely aware of the buildings and structures that surrounded him.

I.M. attended a very strict school. Students had only a half-day off every month. All the lessons were in Chinese, but I.M. also studied English. By the time he was seventeen, he spoke English well. He decided to study architecture in America. In 1935, I.M. set off on the long ocean voyage to the United States.

Eighteen-year-old I.M. embarks for San Francisco on the S.S. Coolidge *in 1935.*

I. M. (front row, third from left) at the Massachusetts Institute of Technology

After a brief stay at the University of
Pennsylvania in Philadelphia, I.M.
transferred to the Massachusetts
Institute of Technology (MIT). There
he was an outstanding architecture
student. At one point, he won a
sketching competition, which
strengthened his interest in drawing.

He also won the American Institute of Architects Medal. In 1940, at the age of twenty-three, he received his bachelor of architecture degree. Later in his life as an architect, I.M. designed four buildings for MIT.

I.M. had intended to return to China as soon as he graduated. But by the time he got his bachelor's degree,

I.M. in Boston in 1936

Years after graduating from MIT, I.M. designed this building for the school—the Weisner Center for Arts, Media and Technology.

Japan had invaded China. I.M.'s father advised him that it would be safer to stay in the United States.

For the next two years, I.M. gained valuable experience working in American cities. In the spring of 1942, he married Eileen Loo, a Wellesley College graduate.

Meanwhile, World War II was raging. In early January of 1943, I.M. volunteered to work for a national defense unit in New Jersey. There he was instructed to design ways to destroy buildings. I.M.'s superiors told him, "If you know how to build a building, you know how to destroy it."

In 1945, I.M. finished his work with national defense. He entered Harvard's Graduate School of Design, which his wife also attended. That same year, Eileen gave birth to their first son, T'ing Chung. I.M. and Eileen later had two more sons, Chien Chung ("Didi") and Li Chung ("Sandi"). Didi and Sandi now work in their father's firm. The youngest child—a daughter named Liane—is an attorney.

While he was still a graduate student, I.M. taught classes at Harvard University. He was deeply impressed

I.M. Pei and his family

by two of his professors at
Harvard—both highly regarded
teachers and architects. One was
Walter Gropius, who had created a
well-known institute of design in
Europe known as the Bauhaus. The
other was Marcel Breuer.

Breuer's influence was especially strong, "particularly his interest in light, texture, sun, and shadow," I.M. has said. In 1952, I.M. designed a home for his family in Katonah, New York. Its glass skylights and partitions clearly show Breuer's influence. I.M. himself gained a reputation on campus as "an elegant designer who would make beautiful things." Since that time, I.M. has known, studied, or taught with many of this century's greatest American and European architects.

After earning his master's degree at Harvard in 1946, I.M. still had hopes of returning to China. But it was not to be. The Communist takeover of his homeland ended that dream. Instead, I.M. went to work as an architect in New York City. Nine years later, in 1955, he became a U.S. citizen. By then he had lived in America nearly twenty years.

In 1955, I.M. established his own architectural firm; here, he meets with the famous New York real estate developer, William Zeckendorf.

The year he became a citizen, I.M. established his own architectural firm in New York City, where he lives and works today. Soon, his flair for dramatic design began to blossom. Glass and concrete were two of his favorite building materials. His designs often included soaring, airy spaces and skylights in vaulted ceilings. His

21

One of Pei's many designs — the Meyerson Symphony Hall in Dallas, Texas

designs were so different—so fresh and imaginative—that it sometimes seemed as if they had been created by many different people rather than just one man. This rich talent and distinctive sense of style attracted the attention of many prominent people.

One such person was Jacqueline Kennedy, the widow of President John F. Kennedy. In 1964, Mrs. Kennedy hired I.M. to design the JFK Memorial Library in Boston. Although the work turned out to be long and difficult, winning this highly prized job was an important step in I.M.'s career. It gave him national recognition and prestige.

A stunning view of Pei's JFK Memorial Library in Boston

In 1979, when the library was finally completed, I. M. received the Gold Medal of the American Institute of Architects, its highest award.

The grace and artistry of I. M.'s designs have brought him many commissions in the Western world. But he has never forgotten his Chinese heritage. He was proud to be asked to design Beijing's Fragrant Hill Hotel.

The interior of the Fragrant Hill Hotel in Beijing, China, in which Pei makes use of natural light through skylights

The soaring glass tower of Pei's Bank of China building in Hong Kong

Another outstanding job was the glittering skyscraper he designed for the Bank of China in Hong Kong. That commission meant a lot to I.M. because it was the bank his father worked for when I.M. was a child.

I. M. has also become extremely well known for his many museum and gallery designs. The most famous may be the design he created for the Louvre in Paris. It is a seven-story steel and glass pyramid. The pyramid—the museum's new entryway—stands in the plaza in front of the Louvre. The pyramid is surrounded by three smaller glass "pyramidons," and at

A scale model of the pyramid Pei designed for the plaza of the Louvre in Paris

Pei rejoiced as construction began on his Louvre pyramid.

night they are lit from within. There
are six hundred light bulbs inside the
large pyramid!

The design caused much argument
at first. The Louvre was once a palace
built for the kings of France. Today it
is perhaps the most famous museum in
the world. Many people thought the
design was inappropriate. Some felt it
was too modern. But many others
delighted in its magical beauty. Soon it

was a welcome new addition to the "City of Light."

The pyramid officially opened in 1989. By then, I.M. was renowned worldwide.

In 1986, at the centennial celebration of the Statue of Liberty, I.M. won the Medal of Liberty. This medal was given to foreign-born U.S. citizens who had made major contributions to American life. I.M. was one of only twelve people to be so honored.

Pei is presented with the Medal of Liberty by Ronald and Nancy Reagan in 1986.

A room in the National Gallery of Art in Washington, D.C.—the ceiling of skylights is an unmistakable I.M. Pei design.

In 1989, he won the $100,000 Praemium Imperiale—an important new award given by the Japanese Art Association. It recognizes lifetime achievement in the arts and is considered the equivalent of the prestigious Nobel Prize.

Today, I.M.'s buildings grace three different continents. He has worked on a grand scale all over the world. His

In 1989, Pei shows his model for the Regent Hotel in New York City.

entire professional life has been devoted to massive, attention-getting buildings. But now he is going in a new direction.

I. M. recently chose to begin designing on a smaller, more personal scale. One of his first designs in this new, scaled-down phase was the Rock 'N' Roll Hall of Fame in Cleveland, Ohio. His new buildings may be smaller, but I.M. is excited and creatively energized by his change of direction. And whatever his direction may be, he seems to live up to his Chinese name: the world is indeed "brightly inscribed" with the works of I.M. Pei.

Pei unveils his model for the Rock 'N' Roll Hall of Fame to Cleveland Mayor George V. Voinovich (right).

I.M. PEI

1917 Born April 26 in Canton, China (now known as Guangzhou)
1918 Moved with family to Hong Kong to escape dangers of fighting warlords in Canton
1927 Moved with family to Shanghai, China
1935 Traveled to America; studied architecture first at the University of Pennsylvania, and then at Massachusetts Institute of Technology (MIT)
1940 Received bachelor of architecture degree from MIT
1942 Married Eileen Loo
1943 Volunteered for a national defense unit in New Jersey during World War II
1945 Entered Harvard Graduate School of Design
1946 Earned master's degree from Harvard
1952 Designed a home for his family in Katonah, New York
1955 Became a United States citizen and established his own architectural firm in New York City
1964 Hired by Mrs. Jacqueline Kennedy to design the JFK Memorial Library in Boston
1979 Completed the JFK Library and was awarded the highest award of the American Institute of Architects, the Gold Medal
1982 Completed Beijing's Fragrant Hill Hotel
1986 Awarded the Medal of Liberty at the centennial celebration of the Statue of Liberty (one of only twelve recipients)
1989 Completed the entryway pyramid of the Louvre art museum in Paris and was awarded the Japanese Art Association's Praemium Imperiale award for lifetime achievement in the arts

INDEX

ABOUT THE AUTHOR

Pamela Dell was born in Idaho, grew up in Chicago, and now lives in Santa Monica, California. At the age of five she decided she should be a writer and began writing stories. In sixth grade, she joined forces with a friend and published her own magazine. Since that encouraging beginning, she has worked as a writer and editor in many different fields and has published nonfiction and short fiction for both adult and young adult readers. She is also the author of *Michael Chang: Tennis Champion*, another Childrens Press Picture-Story Biography.

DATE			